Cows

Jen Green

Grolier
an imprint of

www.scholastic.com/librarypublishing

Published 2009 by Grolier
An Imprint of Scholastic Library Publishing
Old Sherman Turnpike
Danbury, Connecticut 06816

For The Brown Reference Group plc
Project Editor: Jolyon Goddard
Picture Researcher: Clare Newman
Designer: Sarah Williams
Managing Editor: Tim Harris

Volume ISBN-13: 978-0-7172-8039-1
Volume ISBN-10: 0-7172-8039-X

**Library of Congress
Cataloging-in-Publication Data**

Nature's children. Set 5.
   p. cm.
  Includes index.
  ISBN-13: 978-0-7172-8084-1
  ISBN-10: 0-7172-8084-5 (set)
  1. Animals--Encyclopedias, Juvenile. I.
Grolier (Firm)
  QL49.N386 2009
  590.3--dc22
                        2008014674

Printed and bound in China

PICTURE CREDITS

Front Cover: **Shutterstock**: Mark William
Penny.

Back Cover: **Shutterstock**: Clearviewstock,
Tatyana Khramtsova, Robert Soen, TTphoto.

Alamy: Nigel Cattlin 38, Wayne Hutchinson
42; **Photolibrary**: John Carey 37, Oliver
Postgate 6, Tony Robins 41; **Shutterstock**:
Marilyn Barbone 10, Marcus Brown 45, Peter
Clark 2–3, Elnur 5, Karen Givens 18, Grynka
17, Margo Harrison 13, 21, Eric Isselee 4,
Matthew Jacques 34, Laila Kazakevica 33,
David Maska 14, MaxPhoto 26–27, Christian
Musat 9, Mark William Penny 30, Dennis
Albert Richardson 46, Dale A. Stork 22,
Richard Thornton 29.

Contents

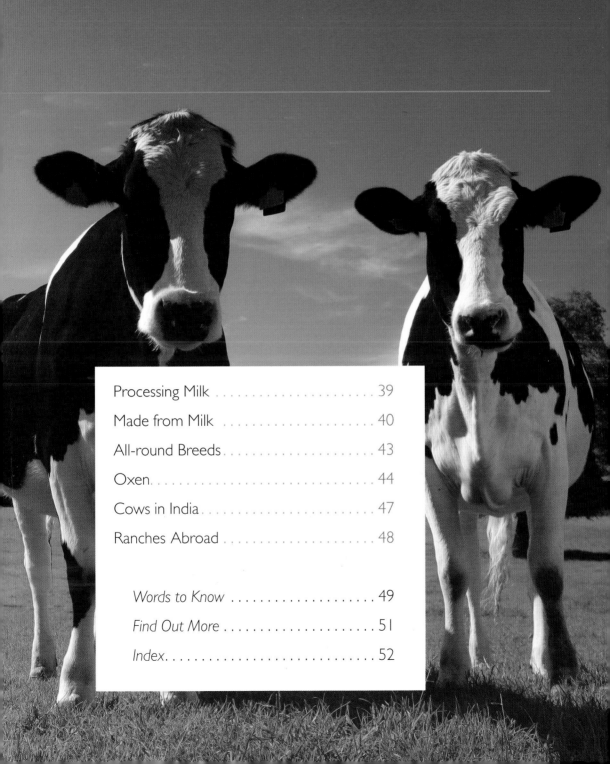

FACT FILE: Cows

Class	Mammals (Mammalia)
Order	Cloven-hoofed mammals (Artiodactyla)
Family	Antelope, cattle, sheep, and goats (Bovidae)
Genus	Yaks, cattle, and other relatives (*Bos*)
Species	Domestic cattle (*Bos taurus*)
World distribution	Most parts of the world
Habitat	Open range or pastureland; a barn may be provided for shelter
Distinctive physical characteristics	Split, or cloven, hooves, a large body, and a long muzzle; many breeds have horns; coat is black, brown, white, or a mixture of those colors
Habits	Cattle graze on pasture and chew the cud; they live in herds
Diet	Grass and other pasture plants, grain, and commercial feed

Introduction

Cows are probably best known for the dairy products made from their milk. Their milk is made into butter, cheese, yogurt, and ice cream.

However, there's a lot more to cows than milk. In many parts of the world, cows or their close relatives are used to plow fields and transport people and goods to market. The word *cow* is just one term for this extremely useful animal. When used correctly, *cow* only applies to the female that produces milk. Cows, **bulls**, or males, and their young, or **calves**, are all cattle.

There are about 1.3 billion cattle in the world today.

5

This photo from 1956 shows a farmer in France using cattle to plow up grapevines. The cattle are blindfolded so that they will not be distracted from their work.

The Useful Cow

People have been raising cows for nearly 10,000 years. Ancient Romans and Egyptians raised cattle for their meat and milk. The cow is one of the most useful farm animals. For this reason, cows are now found in most parts of the world.

In addition to milk, cows are also raised for their meat and their leather hides, which are used to make shoes, belts, and bags. Soap, glue, and medicine also come from the body parts of cows. Big and strong, cattle are used to pull plows and carts. The cattle that do this kind of work are called oxen. Oxen are almost always neutered bulls. Neutering stops animals from being able to breed. It also makes them less aggressive and easier to manage.

When Europeans came to North America, cattle were used to clear the land. They pulled tree stumps out of the ground. They were also used for transport. Pioneers moving west along the Oregon Trail used teams of oxen to pull the wagons that carried families and possessions.

The Cattle Family

Cattle belong to a group of hoofed animals called **bovids**. This family includes yak, bison, and buffalo, as well as **domestic** cattle. More distant relatives include antelope, sheep, goats and gazelles. In total, this large group of mammals contains about 140 different types, or species of animals.

Cattle, bison, and other bovids have a barrel-shaped body and a long **muzzle**. All bovids are plant eaters. They have teeth suited for grinding grass and other plant matter. Their digestive system is also designed to break down, or digest, tough plant food. Bovids live in groups called herds, which provide safety in numbers. In addition, cows and their relatives have horns. They use their horns to defend themselves if an enemy gets too close. Bulls also use their horns to fight one another for cows to **mate** with.

In North America,
the grasslands where
cattle graze are
known as prairies.

9

Highland cattle originate from Scotland. They are a tough breed that can survive in harsh conditions.

History Lesson

Scientists have learned that the first cattlelike animals appeared about 20 million years ago. They know this because of **fossils** that have been found. Modern cattle developed from these early cattle about 2 million years ago. The domestic cattle seen in pastures today are descended from a wild species called the aurochs (OW-RAKS), which roamed Europe and Asia in prehistoric times. However, aurochs died out in the 1600s.

People began to domesticate cattle for meat, milk, and their skin more than 9,000 years ago. As time passed, farmers realized that cattle varied naturally. Some produced a lot of milk, while others were particularly meaty. Farmers began to develop the best milk producers and the best beef cattle separately. Gradually different **breeds** developed. Over the years, breeding has produced hundreds of different types of cattle.

Shape and Size

Cows have a large, bulky body. Adult cattle usually stand about 5 feet (1.5 m) tall and weigh anywhere from 900 to 2,000 pounds (410 to 900 kg). They have squarish hindquarters, and a long tail that they swish to keep pesky flies away. Each of their four feet has two toes that are protected by a horny hoof.

Most cattle are black, white, or brown—or a combination of those colors. The majority of cows have shortish hair that grows a little longer in winter to keep the animals warm. All females have a special organ called an **udder**, which holds milk. The udder hangs down between and just in front of the back legs. Dairy cows are bred to have a larger udder that produces a lot of milk.

Ayrshire cattle are raised for both milk and meat production.

Cows mainly eat grass, but they will occasionally munch on the leaves of other plants, such as dandelions.

14

Plant Eaters

Like all bovids, cattle are **herbivores**, or plant eaters. Cows are **grazers**, mainly feeding on grass. But this coarse food is hard to digest. A cow's stomach has four parts, or chambers. This design allows the animal to easily break down its food.

A grazing cow tears off a mouthful of grass and chews it briefly before swallowing. The swallowed food passes to the first stomach chamber, called the **rumen**, where it is softened. It then passes back to the mouth for a more thorough chewing. That is called chewing the **cud**. Cows spend a lot of time doing that, usually when resting. After this second chewing, the food is swallowed again. This time it passes right through the stomach and intestines, which absorb the nutrients. The cow's complicated digestive system allows it to get the maximum amount of nutrients out of its food. The nutrients allow the cow to grow, and, in the case of dairy cattle, produce milk.

Cow Senses

Both wild and domestic cattle are at risk of being attacked by large predators, such as big cats, wolves, and bears. These predators target young or sick cattle. Cattle, therefore, have good senses that allow them to detect predators early.

Cattle have good eyesight. They can see some colors, but not as many as humans can. With their eyes on the sides of their head, cattle can see almost all around themselves. That is useful for being on the lookout when their head is lowered during grazing. If a cow senses danger, it raises its head to get a better view.

Cattle have sharp hearing. That helps them detect approaching danger and also hear the "moos" of other cattle. Their sense of smell is excellent. Cattle also have a **Jacobson's organ** in their nose. This organ allows them to "taste" chemicals released into the air by other cattle.

Touch is important for cattle. They groom one another to establish bonds. In addition, their skin is sensitive. Cattle can feel the flies that land on them. They use their tail to swish them away.

A cow's large nostrils
help give it a sharp
sense of smell.

17

A Texas longhorn bull's horn tips might be as far as 10 feet (3 m) apart.

The Cattle Industry

Cattle are not found naturally in North America. The first cattle probably arrived with the Vikings, who settled briefly on the east coast about 1,000 years ago. But the first large herd of cattle arrived with the explorer Christopher Columbus, on his second voyage to the Americas in 1493. Not long after, cattle were a common sight in the Spanish colonies throughout the Caribbean.

A few years later, when the Spaniard Hernán Cortés conquered Mexico, he brought cattle to the mainland. From Mexico, cattle soon spread north into Texas and across southwestern North America. Other European settlers also brought cattle. These useful beasts were soon found in every part of the continent except in the icy north.

Beefy Breeds

The United States produces much of the world's beef. Five main breeds of beef cattle are raised in the United States. They are raised in such great numbers that they outnumber dairy cows by four to one.

A breed called the Angus originally came from Scotland. It is prized for its excellent meat. The Brahman was developed from Indian stock. This breed copes well with the heat in southern states. Charolais (SHA-RUH-LAY) cattle from France are large. They are sometimes crossed with other breeds to produce extra-meaty animals. The shorthorn was developed in England as a fast-growing breed. Herefords also came from England. They are one of the most popular breeds in North America. Herefords cope well with cold winters.

Originally from England, the Hereford is now common in the United States, Argentina, Australia, and New Zealand.

A cowhand on horseback separates a cow from the herd. This type of horse riding is called cutting.

Cowhands

By the 1800s, more cattle were being raised in North America than anywhere else in the world. At that time, cattle lived on the wide open range and had to fend for themselves for most of the year. This way of raising cattle saved money for their owner. It also made work for rugged cowhands, who played an important part in building the American West.

Countless movies and television shows have been made about the cowhands' life. However, the reality is a lot less glamorous. A cowhand's day is long and hard, with little time for leisure. These tough people are outdoors in all kinds of weather. They check the livestock and help cows give birth. They round up and **brand** cattle. A cowhand's work might even include chasing off cattle rustlers—people who steal cattle—and the odd prowling cougar.

Cattle Drives

In the days of the open range, cattle from different owners often grazed together. Cowhands branded the livestock in order to tell which cattle belonged to which owner. Each calf was branded with its owner's mark at about one month old. To do that, the cowhands first rounded up the calves. Each animal was then roped, held down, and marked with the hot **branding iron**. Finally, the calves were set free to roam the range.

In the days of the Old West, cowhands had to drive their cattle huge distances to towns with railroads. There, they were loaded on trains bound for the stockyards and slaughterhouses of Chicago. These long and dangerous **cattle drives** could take up to three months and cover as much as 1,000 miles (1,600 km). By the late 1800s, the railroad system had been extended, and the great drives became a thing of the past.

Rodeos

In the days of the Old West, every experienced cowhand was an expert rider. In their free time, cowhands would gather to show off their skills. They would ride, rope, and wrestle cattle to the ground. That's how **rodeos** began.

As rodeos became more popular, they moved to towns. The offer of prize money or trophies, such as silver or gold belt buckles, attracted more competitors. Some cowhands soon became full-time rodeo riders, traveling from show to show to compete.

Modern rodeos have five main events that reflect the skills of the old-time cowhands. These events are bareback **bronco** riding, saddle bronco riding, calf-roping, **steer** wrestling, and bull riding. These exciting events keep the spirit of the old cowhands alive.

A mother cow is very protective of her calf.

Cattle Ranching

The huge farms where cattle are raised are called ranches. On most modern ranches, cattle raising follows a regular pattern. The calves are born in spring. At about one month old, they are branded and then released to graze. The open range is long gone. Modern cattle graze in fenced pastures that are either rented or owned by the ranchers. The young cattle feed and grow through spring and summer.

By fall, the calves have reached 450 to 650 pounds (200 to 300 kg) in weight. They might spend another year on the ranch, or be sold to another rancher for fattening up. After another three to five months, the cattle reach 1,100 pounds (500 kg), and are ready to be sold for meat.

In California, there is often not much grass for cattle to eat. This herd is traveling to a feeding lot, where the ranchers supply them with extra food.

The Holstein is the most common dairy cow in the United States. It originates from Friesland in The Netherlands.

The Dairy Cow

Most mammals produce only enough milk for their young. Dairy cows are different. The average calf needs about 66 gallons (250 l) of its mother's milk as it grows. However, in the ten months after a calf's birth, its mother produces 1,585 gallons (6,000 l) of milk. That's a lot of extra milk that people can use!

The dairy cow needs plenty of food in order to produce so much milk. Each day, she eats about 9 pounds (4 kg) of hay and 35 pounds (16 kg) of **silage**, which is a mixture of grass and grains. She also is given mixed grains, salt, and extra vitamins and minerals.

Dairy Breeds

Modern dairy cattle are the result of centuries of breeding. Dozens of breeds are found around the world, but only five main breeds are commonly raised in the United States.

Holsteins are the most common dairy cattle. They are large with a black-and-white coat. They produce far more milk than any other breed.

The Brown Swiss is one of the oldest breeds of milk cows. In some parts of the world, it is also reared for its meat. Guernsey and Jersey cows originally came from two small islands near France in the English Channel. They are famous for their creamy yellow milk. The fifth main breed of diary cow is the Ayrshire. This rugged breed survives well in hilly country.

Cows feed and rest
in a large, airy barn.

In the United States, California, New York, and Wisconsin produce the most milk.

Dairy Farming

The European settlers who came to North America in the 1600s and 1700s brought dairy cattle with them. Later, pioneer settlers moved west with their cattle. During the 1700s and 1800s, cows were an everyday part of frontier life. As well as providing milk and beef, they also pulled wagons and plows.

From the 1800s onward, cities began to spring up all over the United States. The large numbers of people living in the cities still wanted milk, butter, and cheese, but they had no space to keep cows. Dairy farms were established on the outskirts of cities to provide milk for the city dwellers.

Modern dairy farms are much more efficient than the old-time farms. Farmers use modern equipment to get the most out of their stock. Most dairy farmers belong to an organization called a cooperative, which helps them get the best price for their milk.

Modern Milking

In the past, cows were milked by hand, which took a long time. Today, machines do most of the milking. Milking machines can service several cows at once. They are also cleaner and gentler than human hands.

Milking machines have several sets of four teat cups—one for each teat on the cow's udder. The udders are carefully washed and disinfected, then a teat cup is hooked onto each teat. A gentle pulling motion draws the milk out of the cow. Cows are usually milked twice a day. A cow produces milk for ten months after her calf is born. Then she must mate again and birth another calf in order to continue to produce milk.

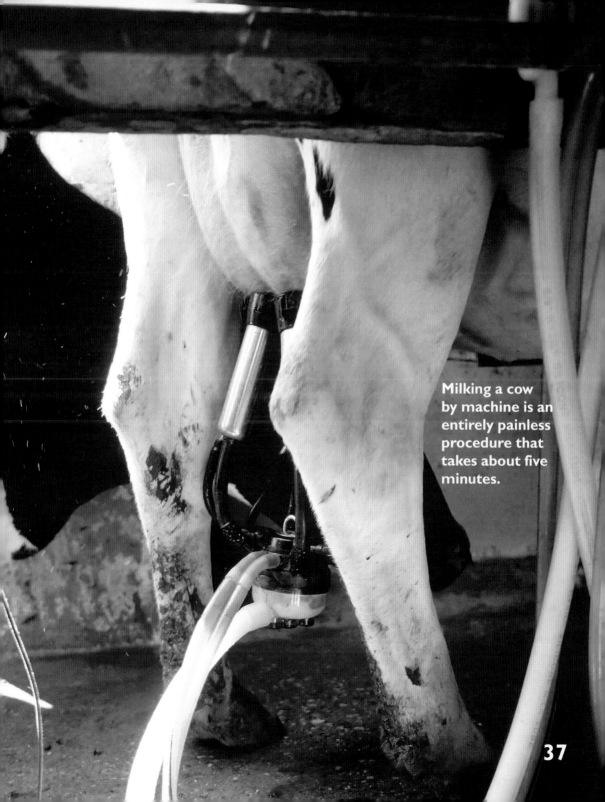

Milking a cow by machine is an entirely painless procedure that takes about five minutes.

Inside a dairy, hygiene is very important.

Processing Milk

When dairy cows are milked, the milk passes
straight into a refrigerated, or cooled, tank.
That will keep the milk fresh. Every day or
so, it is trucked from the farm to the dairy.
There, it is carefully checked and processed
to make sure it is safe to drink.

Like all natural products, cow's milk may
contain **bacteria**—the microscopic germs that
can cause illness. A process called **pasteurization**
removes the bacteria from the milk. The milk is
heated to at least 160°F (72°C) for 16 seconds or
more, and then cooled. That gets rid of any
germs, and the milk is then safe to drink.

Most milk then goes through a second
process called **homogenization**. This process
breaks down the natural milk fat, which makes
the milk smoother. Some of the milk fat might
then be skimmed off. Vitamins may also be added
to make the milk even more nutritious for people.
The result is delicious, cool, frothy milk!

Made from Milk

Less than 40 percent of cow's milk is actually sold as milk. The majority of milk is used to make products such as butter, cheese, buttermilk, yogurt, and ice cream.

To make butter, cream is pasteurized and then stirred, or churned. During churning, the milk fat becomes more and more solid. Eventually it turns to creamy butter. Cheese is made by adding helpful bacteria to milk, which causes soft **curds** to form. These curds are strained off and become cheese.

Ice cream is made by blending milk and sugar. The mixture is pasteurized and homogenized, and then flavoring is mixed in. Air bubbles are also added to make the mixture smooth and creamy. It is then frozen. Finally chunks of nuts, fruit, cookies, or chocolate are added. With all those goodies, it's not surprising that ice cream is many people's favorite milk product!

Dairy produce isn't for everyone—the sugars and proteins found in milk can cause illness in some people.

A newborn shorthorn
calf heads for its mother's
udder to drink as soon as
it can stand up.

All-round Breeds

In the days of ancient Rome and Egypt, cattle were all-rounders. They were raised to yield both meat and milk. They also pulled carts and plows. Some modern breeds are also raised for both beef and milk, though many farmers and ranchers prefer specialized breeds.

A breed of cow called the milking shorthorn is a common sight all over the Midwest and the eastern United States. These cattle produce large amounts of beef and milk. The red poll is another popular all-rounder. This breed was first developed in England. Red polls have a deep red coat, sometimes with a white tail, and do not grow horns. A **polled** animal is one without horns.

Oxen

Oxen have been raised for thousands of years. They are usually neutered males. A neutered male is known as a steer. Oxen are the biggest cattle, with a large head, heavy body, and strong muscles. These powerful beasts are still used to pull plows and wagons in many parts of the world.

In the United States, oxen are no longer used for hauling. However, some are still kept on farms. No county or state fair would be complete without an ox-pulling contest! Teams of oxen compete to see which can pull the heaviest load. A well-trained team can move up to 3,000 pounds (1,350 kg) loaded on a sled. When not pulling, these beasts can be seen peacefully grazing in the meadows.

A team of oxen pulls a farmer's cart in Myanmar, a country in Southeast Asia.

A sacred cow in
India is adorned
with a bell and
painted horns.

Sacred Cows

India probably has more cows than any other country in the world. Yet very few of them end up as meat. That is because most people in India are Hindus. Their religion, Hinduism, teaches that animals, as well as humans, have souls. To many Hindus, cows are sacred. For this reason, these animals are carefully tended. Even the thought of eating meat from a cow is shocking to some Hindus. At religious festivals, people place strings of flowers around the necks of cattle.

Cattle are still very important to farming in India. Cows yield milk, and both cows and bulls are still used for plowing and transport. A team of long-horned cattle pulling a plow is a familiar sight in the Indian countryside.

Ranches Abroad

Cattle ranches are not just found in the United States. The dry grasslands of Australia are home to many cattle, too. Life on these rugged grasslands is as rough and tough as it is on any ranch in the American West.

In the far south of Argentina, in South America, the grassy plains called the pampas (PAM-PUSS) are also famous for cattle ranching. The cowhands there are called gauchos (GOW-CHOZE), and they are as important to Argentinian folklore as the cowhands of North America are to American folklore.

North of Argentina, cattle ranching is big business in Venezuela. Most ranches are found on the grassy meadowlands called the llanos (LAH-NOZE).

Wherever cows are raised, they are a much valued and respected farm animal. Their strength, their milk, and other products have helped humans survive for thousands of years—and will certainly continue to do so for very many years to come.

Words to Know

Bacteria	Microscopic living things that can cause disease.
Bovids	Members of the cattle family.
Brand	To mark in order to identify the owner of an animal.
Branding iron	The tool used to brand cattle.
Breeds	Types of a domestic animal.
Bronco	A wild horse that has not been broken in for riding.
Bulls	Adult male cattle.
Calves	Young cattle.
Cattle drives	When cattle were driven to the railroad to be transported to stockyards or slaughterhouses.
Cud	A lumpy mass of partly digested food that is chewed again by cattle.
Curds	A semisolid food formed from milk that is used to make cheese.
Domestic	Tamed and raised by humans.

Fossils	The preserved remains of ancient animals and plants.
Grazers	Animals that eat mainly grass.
Herbivores	Animals that eat plants, not meat.
Homogenization	Making milk smoother by breaking up its fat content.
Jacobson's organ	An structure in a cow's nose that can "taste" chemicals in the air.
Mate	To come together to produce young.
Muzzle	The jaws and nose of an animal.
Pasteurization	When milk is processed by heating it to kill harmful bacteria.
Polled	Describing cattle that lack horns.
Rodeos	Contests that test the skills of cowhands, such as lassoing calves and riding broncos.
Rumen	One of the four stomach chambers of a cow.
Silage	Feed for cattle.
Steer	A bull that has been neutered.
Udder	The part of a cow that holds the milk.

Find Out More

Books

Miller, S. S. *Cows*. True Books: Animals. Danbury, Connecticut: Children's Press, 2000.

Steele, C. *Cattle Ranching in the American West*. America's Westward Expansion. Milwaukee, Wisconsin: World Almanac Library, 2005.

Web sites

Cow
www.enchantedlearning.com/subjects/mammals/farm/Cowprintout.shtml
Facts about cows and a printout to color in.

Cow Power
kids.nationalgeographic.com/Stories/SpaceScience/Cow-power
Learn about making electricity from cow manure!

Index